Adventures of
Stella & Macie

Inspired by a True Story

Written By:
Erica Merlis

Illustrated By:
Monique Romischer

Halo
PUBLISHING
INTERNATIONAL

Adventures of Stella & Macie:
Inspired by a True Story
Copyright © 2021 Erica Merlis
Illustrated by Monique Romischer
All rights reserved.

ISBN: 978-1-61244-983-8
LCCN: 2021904555

Halo Publishing International, LLC
8000 W Interstate 10, Suite 600
San Antonio, Texas 78230
www.halopublishing.com

Printed and bound in the United States of America

Thank you to Stella and Macie for inspiring me to write this book about the whimsical dreams of a four-year-old girl.

To my family: Brent, Caden, Tyler and Stella–thank you for making me smile, scream, laugh and cry while always appreciating the life we have together.

To my Mom, Dad and sister, Stefanie–thank you for showing me what a great family we have, one I try to model for my own. Growing up with cats, parakeets, bunnies and our family dog, Susie, was something special.

Love you all!

Introduction

"Mommy, when will the Coronavirus be over?" said Stella, a four-year-old little girl with long, curly brown hair, brown eyes and big dimples.

Due to the Coronavirus, Stella and her brothers, Caden and Tyler had been home for months. Life with no school, no activities, and only seeing friends from a distance was hard. The Coronavirus, also known as COVID-19, was spreading and causing people to have a cough, fever, sore throat and problems breathing.

"Stella, I'm not sure how long this will last," her mommy said. "To be safe, when we leave the house, we need to wear our masks, try to stay six feet apart from people, sanitize our hands often and then, when we come home, wash our hands very well."

Pet Store

"Mommy, Mommy, when can we go to the pet store? I want to see the puppies playing and jumping. It is so funny watching their heads go up and down, and up and down," Stella said in a giggling voice.

After weeks of Stella asking, her mommy finally agreed to take her to the pet store. Stella put on her favorite purple rainbow unicorn mask, and off they went.

Stella was so excited as she walked into the pet store. Even her mommy looked forward to seeing the puppies again. But, to their surprise, there were NO puppies.

"Mommy, there are NO PUPPIES! Where did they all go?"

"Sorry, Stella," said the pet store owner. "They have all been sold."

"SOLD! How can they ALL be sold?" Stella said.

The store owner explained that due to the Coronavirus, many people were staying at home and wanted to have a puppy become part of their families.

Week after week, Stella and her mommy visited the pet store, only to see the big sign on the window that read NO PUPPIES.

That gave her mommy an idea. The next time they went to the pet store, she showed Stella other animals that were available like guinea pigs, fish and bunny rabbits.

"What about a guinea pig like Bingo?" her mommy said.

Stella's brother, Caden, had the sweetest guinea pig with fluffy brown and white fur. Bingo loved rolling around inside his large green ball and playing hide and seek in his little house. Stella's mommy thought getting her a guinea pig could be a great choice, but Stella said, "No, Mommy, I really want a puppy."

"How about fish?" said her mommy. Her brothers, Caden and Tyler won Superhero and Ninja at a local carnival, and they loved watching them swim around and pucker up for food. Superhero and Ninja were both orange and gold. Even though they were the same color, they were easy to tell apart. Superhero had some black spots on him, and Ninja had olive-green spots.

Stella shook her head. "No, Mommy, I really want a puppy."

Then her mommy suggested a bunny rabbit. "When I was a little girl, we had bunnies. They were so cute; they would hop around everywhere. Sometimes, they were so fast that we could not catch them."

"No, Mommy, I really want a puppy," said Stella.

Stella's Promise

Every day, Stella told her mommy, "Mommy, I promise if I get a puppy, I will feed it and play with it, and hug it and sing it songs." But there were still NO PUPPIES for sale.

Stella's Dream

One spring morning, Stella woke up and said, "Mommy, I had a dream that we bought Daddy a puppy for Father's Day."

"Really?" her mommy said.

"Oh, Mommy, please, please can we just check one more time," said Stella.

"Ok, Stella," Mommy said. "Let's put on our masks and go to the pet store one last time."

Stella's Dream Comes True!

Stella and her mommy went back to the pet store. "Mommy, I don't see the No Puppies sign," Stella said, pointing at the window. Stella ran by the guinea pigs. She ran by the fish. She ran by the bunnies. Suddenly, they heard squeaky little barks. "Mommy, I hear puppies!"

Stella ran to where the puppies were and saw three little puppies with pink bows named Macie, Mia and McKenzie. Stella's eyes lit up. The puppies jumped up and down, and so did Stella. "Mommy, these are the cutest puppies I have ever seen."

Macie, Mia and McKenzie were sisters. They looked like teddy bears with their red, soft, curly fur.

There was something very special about the way Stella looked at Macie. "Mommy, Mommy, I want that one. Oh please, can I have her? Look at her cute little white stripe all the way from her face down to her belly. And Mommy, look at her two little white paws."

Mommy said, "Come here, Stella. Come sit in this room." The room was bright yellow with only one pink chair, perfect for Stella to sit on. Stella sat down, and the pet store owner put Macie on Stella's lap. Stella hugged her and snuggled her and gave her lots of kisses.

The Big Surprise

Stella and Mommy arrived home to surprise
Daddy with Macie. "Daddy! I'm finally a big sister."

18

Stella and Her Best Friend Macie

Every morning around 6:30, Stella woke up to Macie's little squeaky bark that grew louder and louder-woof, Woof, WOOF!

"Here I come," said Stella, as she jumped out of her bed and ran downstairs to open Macie's crate. Macie almost knocked Stella over with the sweetest and sloppiest kisses. Stella giggled and giggled. "I love you Macie, you are my best friend."

Going to the Playground

Stella and Macie loved spending time together.

"Macie, Macie, it's time to go to the playground," said Stella. Stella could not wait to climb the rock wall. Whatever Stella tried to do, Macie followed. "Macie, you silly little puppy, you can't climb the rock wall." While Stella climbed higher and higher, Macie's squeaky bark became really loud. "I did it," Stella yelled from the top of the wall. "Don't worry Macie. Now it's your turn. Let's go over to the slide."

Stella climbed a few steps to get to the top of the purple slide. Then her mommy placed Macie on her lap. Stella gave Macie a tight squeeze, and as they went down the slide she shouted, "Here we go!"

"Woof, woof, WOOOOOOOF," Macie barked.

"Macie, you're so much fun to be with," said Stella.

September

Stella and Macie spent every day together until the beginning of September. Then Stella and her brothers went back to school. Stella, Macie, and her brothers waited for the school bus. As the boys went on, so did Macie.

"No, Macie," Mommy said. "The bus is only for kids, not puppies."

"Your turn, Stella." Mommy put Stella in her car seat. Macie had her own car seat too. When they arrived at school, Stella gave Macie a huge hug, hopped out of the car, and ran into school.

When they got home, Macie whined and searched the empty house. Where was everyone?

Mommy said, "Macie, I promise you more fun in the afternoon. For now, enjoy your bone and dog bed, and take a nice nap." That is exactly what Macie did.

In the afternoon, Mommy and Macie went to school to pick up Stella and her brothers. As soon as Macie saw Stella, she ran into her arms. She gave her a giant puppy hug and licked her face all over.

Stella hugged her back. "I love you Macie, you are my best friend."

CPSIA information can be obtained
at www.ICGtesting.com
Printed in the USA
BVHW051927060721
611238BV00021B/1247

9 781612 449838